G000058586

BE KIND

SOPHIE GOLDING

summersdale

BE KIND

Copyright © Summersdale Publishers Ltd, 2020

All rights reserved.

No part of this book may be reproduced by any means, nor transmitted, nor translated into a machine language, without the written permission of the publishers.

Condition of Sale
This book is sold subject to the condition that it shall not, by way of trade or otherwise, be lent, resold, hired out or otherwise circulated in any form of binding or cover other than that in which it is published and without a similar condition including this condition being imposed on the subsequent purchaser.

An Hachette UK Company
www.hachette.co.uk

Summersdale Publishers Ltd
Part of Octopus Publishing Group Limited
Carmelite House
50 Victoria Embankment
LONDON
EC4Y 0DZ
UK

www.summersdale.com

Printed and bound in the Czech Republic

ISBN: 978-1-78783-817-8

Substantial discounts on bulk quantities of Summersdale books are available to corporations, professional associations and other organizations. For details contact general enquiries: telephone: +44 (0) 1243 771107 or email: enquiries@summersdale.com.

INTRODUCTION

Kindness is a type of magic you can keep in your pocket and sprinkle at will – and best of all, it's free! The joy and positivity that a small act of kindness releases into the world is contagious; one act of kindness *always* sparks another. And when people actively go the extra mile to make their community a better place, it can start a chain of compassion that echoes around the world.

This little book is packed full of uplifting stories of genuine acts of selfless kindness from all over the globe, as well as ideas for ways you can spread goodwill in your everyday life, either to your loved ones or to complete strangers. You don't need huge amounts of money or any fancy equipment; all you need is a heart, a little bit of time and good intentions. We hope this book serves as a small but mighty reminder of the good that humans are capable of when they put their minds to it.

#BEKIND

NO ACT
OF KINDNESS,
HOWEVER
SMALL, IS EVER
WASTED.

AESOP

When Andi Bernabe was summoned by his friends on his eighteenth birthday, he didn't realize the surprise he was in for. The trans teenager was unaware that his classmates had spent the last month saving up money for him to be able to change his name legally. They sang "Happy Birthday" and presented him with an envelope containing $300, along with a homemade birth certificate bearing his new name. What an incredible show of love and support for a friend.

KINDNESS IS THE CHEAPEST, MOST REWARDING GIFT YOU CAN GIVE TO SOMEONE ELSE

THOSE WHO
BRING SUNSHINE
TO THE LIVES OF
OTHERS CANNOT
KEEP IT FROM
THEMSELVES.

J. M. BARRIE

Ways to be kind

Say "thank you"! Those small words really are powerful, and can make people feel so much more seen and appreciated. Whether you're thanking your loved ones for the things they do to enrich your life, or simply making an effort to acknowledge the staff in your local shop or in a call centre, a "thank you" is never wasted.

As the sun makes ice melt, kindness causes misunderstanding, mistrust and hostility to evaporate.

ALBERT SCHWEITZER

When 13-year-old Callum Manning first set up an Instagram account to post his book reviews, he was bullied by some of his classmates who left mean comments. His sister tweeted about the event, hoping to find him some more support – and he got it. Within a few days, Callum had more than 80,000 new followers, and messages of encouragement from booksellers, authors, readers and celebrities from across the world.

Make
someone
happy
today

THREE THINGS
IN HUMAN LIFE ARE
IMPORTANT. THE FIRST IS
TO BE KIND. THE SECOND
IS TO BE KIND. AND THE
THIRD IS TO BE KIND.

HENRY JAMES

Ways to be kind

Why not volunteer at your local care home or with a charity that helps the elderly? Many senior citizens struggle with loneliness, so arranging a regular phone call or visit is a lovely way to brighten someone's day. As they say, strangers are just friends you haven't met yet – it may lead to a deep and fulfilling new friendship for both of you.

Remember there's no such thing as a small act of kindness. Every act creates a ripple with no logical end.

SCOTT ADAMS

After being in hospital for days with her ill nine-week-old son, a young mother in Canberra, Australia was met with a parking ticket on her car windscreen. On opening up the envelope to see how much she had been fined, she noticed a pink note attached to the paperwork. The note was from a stranger called Laura, who wanted to let the young mother know that she had already paid the fine on her behalf. It was just the boost the family needed.

SPREAD
YOUR
LOVE TO
EVERYONE

Gentleness and kindness will make our homes a paradise upon earth.

C. A. BARTOL

Ways to be kind

Offer your help to friends. Maybe you know a new parent who hasn't had any time to look after themselves and would benefit from an hour or two of babysitting. Or perhaps a friend has moved house and would appreciate the offer to help them decorate. Take a moment to think about how you could make a positive difference to your loved ones.

THE WORDS
OF KINDNESS
ARE MORE
HEALING TO A
DROOPING HEART
THAN BALM
OR HONEY.

SARAH FIELDING

Aaron Collins loved to give big tips to waiting staff and see the unexpected joy it brought people. His generosity in life continued after he died at the age of 30, as his family carried out his final wish of giving a waiter a $500 tip. The video of the occasion prompted donations to roll in to the cause, enabling Aaron's family to keep giving unexpecting waiting staff the tip of their life. You can find out more at aaroncollins.org. What a legacy to leave behind.

WE BECOME
HAPPIER
BY MAKING
OTHERS HAPPY

HE WHO SOWS
COURTESY
REAPS FRIENDSHIP,
AND HE WHO
PLANTS KINDNESS
GATHERS LOVE.

SAINT BASIL

Ways to be kind

Send someone you love a care package. Think about what they'll really appreciate – a journal to start planning that novel they've always talked about? A packet of seeds for them to plant in their herb garden? A pair of cosy socks and a DVD so they can have a movie night at home? Or just a handwritten letter, letting them know you're thinking about them. Whatever you send, it's bound to make their day.

*What sunshine
is to flowers,
smiles are
to humanity.*

JOSEPH ADDISON

When a bookshop in Southampton, UK, needed to relocate to a new building 150 metres down the road, it called upon its loyal customers and members of the local community to help them move their stock. More than 250 people turned up to help, meaning they could create a human chain from the old shop to the new premises and make light work of the move. To cap it off, the shop turned its first floor into accommodation for homeless people in the area.

STEP OUT OF YOUR COMFORT ZONE AND GIVE A STRANGER THE GIFT OF KINDNESS

A SINGLE ACT
OF KINDNESS THROWS
OUT ROOTS IN ALL
DIRECTIONS, AND THE
ROOTS SPRING UP AND
MAKE NEW TREES.

AMELIA EARHART

Ways to be kind

Send someone flowers, for no reason. (Chocolate cake also works well, if they're not a flower person.) You'll be surprised how much this small gesture can brighten someone's day.

Genuine kindness
is no ordinary
act, but a gift of
rare beauty.

SYLVIA ROSSETTI

Since 1995, American Mohamed Bzeek has fostered over 40 children. Inspired by his Muslim faith, he does it to help those who need support the most. And for him, nationality, religion and what country the children come from are of no importance: "To me it doesn't matter, I do it as a human being for another human being." An inspiring man with a heart of gold.

We
grow by
helping
others
grow

If the only prayer you said in your whole life was "thank you", that would suffice.

MEISTER ECKHART

Ways to be kind

Being kind isn't always about taking the initiative yourself. Look around you and you'll find like-minded people looking for ways to improve the world. Why not help by amplifying their message? Spread the word about people running fundraisers or awareness campaigns and you'll help their light of positivity shine even brighter.

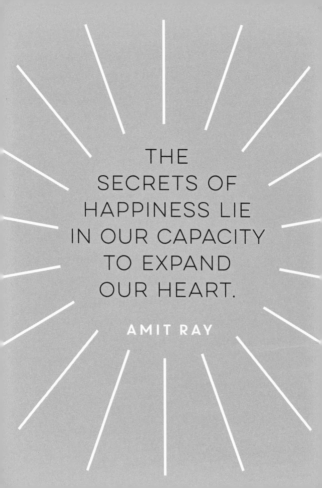

THE
SECRETS OF
HAPPINESS LIE
IN OUR CAPACITY
TO EXPAND
OUR HEART.

AMIT RAY

When six-year-old Vincent Butterfield found out that his best friend had leukaemia, he did everything in his power to make him feel normal. As well as donating $200 to help his friend's family pay for treatment, he shaved his head so that his best friend would "feel like he's not the only one without any hair". What a selfless act that demonstrates friendship at its strongest.

A SMILE A DAY KEEPS THE DOCTOR AWAY

IF YOU
WANT TO
BE A REBEL,
BE KIND.

NIPUN MEHTA

Ways to be kind

You can spread kindness in a more practical way by donating to food banks. Most supermarkets have donation boxes, and if not you'll probably find a food bank nearby that you can donate to directly. Most places will accept any long-life food such as tinned and dry goods like pasta, rice or dried fruit, but they may also be on the lookout for household items such as cleaning supplies, toiletries and sanitary products.

*The wonderful
thing is that it's so
incredibly easy
to be kind.*

INGRID NEWKIRK

Ollie Jones of Exmouth, UK, told his mum he was very excited about opening the birthday cards he'd receive for his soon-approaching fifteenth birthday. His mum, knowing he didn't have many friends and worried that he wouldn't receive anything, sent a plea on Facebook to ask the community for help. What she didn't expect was the amazing response from complete strangers. On his birthday, Ollie received around 20,000 cards, messages and presents from people all over the world. Now that's cause for celebration!

KINDNESS
IS A GIFT
EVERYONE
CAN AFFORD
TO GIVE

LOOK FOR A WAY TO
LIFT SOMEONE UP. AND
IF THAT'S ALL YOU DO,
THAT'S ENOUGH.

ELIZABETH LESSER

Ways to be kind

Make an effort to remember the important things going on in your friends' and colleagues' lives. If someone tells you they have an exam or a big presentation at work coming up, for instance, set a reminder on your phone so you can send them a message of support in the morning and let them know you're sending them good vibes. It might just be the boost they need.

Kindness is a language which the deaf can hear and the blind can see.

ANONYMOUS

Since 2015, Josh Coombes, from Devon, UK, has been giving free haircuts to the homeless. His #DoSomethingForNothing initiative has gained over 60,000 Instagram followers and his vision is all about "sharing love through uncertain times". He has also teamed up with Jade Statt, founder of StreetVet, who provides support for homeless people's furry friends. Now that's one kind double act.

THERE'S SO MUCH TO GAIN FROM THE ACT OF GIVING

A smile is
happiness
you'll find right
under your nose.

TOM WILSON

Ways to be kind

Shop local! Whether they're greengrocers, hardware stores or art supply stockists, the quality of the products you buy and the customer service you receive is nearly always higher when you buy from local, independent stores. Supporting small businesses helps the local community and your money will be genuinely appreciated.

KINDNESS
IS ALWAYS
FASHIONABLE,
AND ALWAYS
WELCOME.

AMELIA BARR

When Andy Mitchell spotted a man walking on the side of the road in 35°C (95°F) heat, he stopped to offer him a ride. It transpired that the man, Justin, walked three miles to work every day in the scorching heat because he couldn't afford a car, but depended on his job. Andy posted about Justin's story on social media that night and, before long, local business owners came together to raise enough money to provide Justin with a car, a year of insurance, two years of oil changes and $500 of fuel.

Sow
kindness
and
reap the
benefits

A KIND AND
COMPASSIONATE
ACT IS OFTEN ITS
OWN REWARD.

WILLIAM JOHN BENNETT

Ways to be kind

Have a clear-out! This is great for you and your cupboards, but it also means that you can take a big bag full of donations to your local charity shop. If you're like most people, you'll probably have loads of things in perfectly good condition lying around that you just don't use. One man's trash...

We make a living
by what we get,
but we make a life
by what we give.

ANONYMOUS

YouTube prankster and social experimentalist Riceman was shown kindness at its most sincere in one of his vlogs. He spotted a homeless man holding up a sign and, in exchange for a couple of coins, asked if the homeless man could offer any information on his missing brother. Riceman left but, instead of going back to pleading for money, the homeless man held up the poster of the missing brother for passers-by to see. When asked why he did it, the guy responded, "What kind of a person would I be if I didn't help someone else?" Selflessness at its best.

ENJOY THE FEELING THAT BEING KIND BRINGS

HOW CAN THERE BE
MORE MEANING THAN
HELPING ONE ANOTHER
STAND UP IN A WIND
AND STAY WARM?

ANNE LAMOTT

Ways to be kind

Organize a fundraiser for a cause that's close to your heart. Maybe you could set up a bake sale (who doesn't love cake?!) or, if you have a particular talent, why not auction off your skills to the highest bidder, and send the proceeds to a charity or local organization? They will be able to do untold good with what you've given.

You cannot do a
kindness too soon,
for you never
know how soon it
will be too late.

RALPH WALDO EMERSON

Christie Dietz's four-year-old son rode his bike every day and would always park it by the same lamppost. The bike was bright green and very distinctive, so locals would always recognize it. One day, Christie and her son arrived at the lamppost to discover that someone had put a "parking bay" sticker on it – underneath the parking sign was a picture of her son's green bike and the word "only". The sweet gesture put a smile on everyone's face.

ON A DREARY DAY,
SHARE YOUR
SUNSHINE
WITH OTHERS

Kind words
do not cost
much. Yet they
accomplish much.

BLAISE PASCAL

Ways to be kind

Reach out to someone you haven't heard from in a while. Make the effort to send a text, write a postcard or make a call. They may be going through a rough time, but even if they're not, they're bound to appreciate the fact that you thought of them.

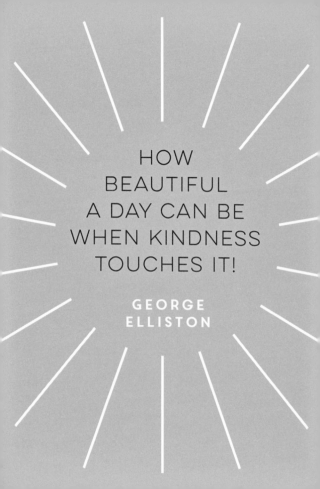

HOW
BEAUTIFUL
A DAY CAN BE
WHEN KINDNESS
TOUCHES IT!

GEORGE
ELLISTON

When Mark Chalifoux was mistakenly added to a WhatsApp group, an accident turned into a heart-warming story. He saw that a family were organizing a care package for a relative serving in the military and, instead of leaving the group, he set up an online fundraising page to help. The page gained momentum, and Mark was able to send 18 kg (40 lb) of cookies as well as a package of essentials to the soldier. The best part? He's still in touch with the family today.

FIND JOY IN EVERYTHING YOU DO AND PASS THAT JOY ON TO OTHERS

KINDNESS IS
MORE IMPORTANT
THAN WISDOM,
AND THE
RECOGNITION
OF THIS IS THE
BEGINNING
OF WISDOM.

THEODORE ISAAC RUBIN

Ways to be kind

Be the person who helps that stranger who is clearly struggling. When a parent is battling to get a stroller up the stairs, or someone is carrying huge bags of groceries to their car, offer a hand. The psychology of crowds makes it easy for most people to avoid taking actions to help, as we assume someone else will, or it's "not our problem", but it's nearly always appreciated by the recipient, and it may encourage them to do the same for someone else next time...

It is only with gratitude that life becomes rich.

DIETRICH BONHOEFFER

In 2018, an IKEA store in Catania, Italy, officially opened its doors to the city's stray dog population. After a customer spotted a few lounging pups on the store's furniture displays, staff decided to allow them in as permanent residents. The dogs are now housed, fed and cared for by the IKEA staff, and are sometimes even adopted by customers who can't imagine their interiors without a furry friend! What a way to spread paws-itivity!

A little bit of love goes a long, long way

BE HONEST,
BE KIND,
AND SHARE
THE LOVE.

SUZI QUATRO

Ways to be kind

When was the last time you let the people in your life know how much you appreciate them? There might be a handful of people who don't immediately come to mind — perhaps a colleague at work who is always happy to offer their time to help you out, or maybe the barista at your favourite coffee shop who always serves you with a smile. Write them a letter to let them know how much you value their kindness, and you'll be helping keep the cogs of kindness turning.

What wisdom can you find that is greater than kindness?

JEAN-JACQUES ROUSSEAU

The Big Green Bookshop, based in the UK, runs a weekly #BuyAStrangerABookDay, and anyone can join in. People volunteer to buy books for total strangers, and the bookshop also donates a number of books every week. Sometimes the recipient has requested a certain book, other times the buyer chooses one they think will help others, and often the bookshop donates books to schools – either way, it results in a lot of very happy people as the joy of knowing you've spread the love with a book is almost better than getting a book yourself! Join in the fun at biggreenbookshop.com or on Twitter @Biggreenbooks.

GIVE TO THOSE WHO NEED IT MOST

The problem with people is they forget that most of the time it's the small things that count.

JENNIFER NIVEN

Ways to be kind

Sign up to a pen-pal site that can pair you with someone who is feeling lonely, be it an older person suddenly living alone, a disadvantaged child, or even someone in prison. Receiving a handwritten letter from a kind stranger may be the thing that makes their day, or even their week — and you may also open a window into a world you'd otherwise have never discovered.

SOMETIMES IT
TAKES ONLY ONE
ACT OF KINDNESS
AND CARING
TO CHANGE A
PERSON'S LIFE.

JACKIE CHAN

When a woman in the US snapped at a barista at a Starbucks drive-thru, no one thought it out of the ordinary. However, only the next day the same woman returned with a note of apology and a $50 tip, letting the barista know how much she regretted her behaviour. The woman also thanked the barista, for their hard work and their determination, and for teaching her about compassion. After all, it's never too late to be kind.

SPREAD
NOTHING BUT
GOOD VIBES
TODAY

DO THINGS
FOR PEOPLE
NOT BECAUSE
OF WHO THEY
ARE OR WHAT
THEY DO IN
RETURN, BUT
BECAUSE OF
WHO YOU ARE.

HAROLD S. KUSHNER

Ways to be kind

Compliment a stranger. It could be on the shoes they're wearing, how contagious their smile is or how much you like their outfit. Think about how good it feels to know you've been noticed in a positive way, and then give that gift to someone else. Compliments are free to hand out, so give them out whenever you can.

*Love and kindness
are never wasted.
They always make a
difference. They bless
the one who receives
them, and they bless
you, the giver.*

BARBARA DE ANGELIS

After trawling through endless websites and magazines, a teenager in Essex, UK, collected enough supermarket coupons to buy £600 worth of shopping for 4p. Having perfected the art of "couponing" through months of helping his mother get by on her limited salary, Jordan planned a shop for a very special occasion. Deciding that he wanted to help as many people as he could with his voucher-hunting skills, Jordan donated all of the food to charity, to help feed disadvantaged families at Christmas.

ENJOY THE
HAPPINESS
YOU CREATE
WHEN YOU
OFFER
SOMEONE A
COMPLIMENT

KNOW HOW TO GIVE
WITHOUT HESITATION,
HOW TO LOSE WITHOUT
REGRET, HOW TO ACQUIRE
WITHOUT MEANNESS.

GEORGE SAND

Ways to be kind

Why don't you consider some random acts of kindness for the planet too? Challenge yourself to do something kind for the environment by walking or biking instead of travelling by car, using a reusable water bottle or coffee cup, or picking up any litter you come across on your outdoor excursions. These little acts will not only make you feel great – the environment will flourish from your selfless acts too.

Wherever there
is a human being,
there is an
opportunity for
a kindness.

SENECA

In 2015, nine-year-old Marlee Pack found out that she had a rare form of soft tissue cancer, which led to weeks of exhausting chemotherapy. When Marlee was well enough to return to school, she was worried that her shaved head would make her stand out. That's where her friend Cameron McLaughlin stepped in, shaving her head in solidarity and encouraging around 80 others at the school to do the same. In the process, the school raised more than $25,000 for a childhood cancer research organization.

Sleep.
Eat.
Be kind.
Repeat.

**Kindness
is like snow –
it beautifies
everything
it covers.**

KAHLIL GIBRAN

Ways to be kind

Take the time today to really listen to someone you don't always see eye to eye with, and maybe you'll even get to understand them better in the process. It's all too easy to brush off the people we don't consider part of our "inner circle", but try to take the time to have a real conversation with that colleague or housemate — to ask them about themselves, find out about their likes and dislikes, and really *listen* to the answers. Giving someone the time and permission to open up could be the key to a new friendship.

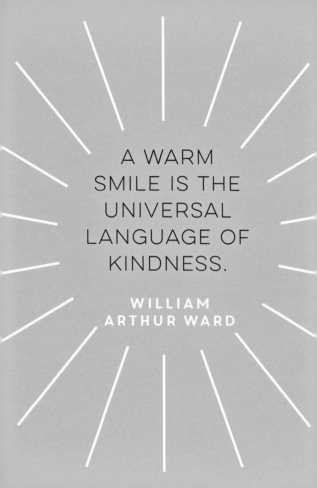

A WARM SMILE IS THE UNIVERSAL LANGUAGE OF KINDNESS.

WILLIAM ARTHUR WARD

The children at the Children's Hospital Colorado had all their superhero dreams come true in 2016, when the state's police department decided to dress up as best-loved characters, such as Iron Man, Spider-Man and Captain America. Dangling from harnesses, the police officers made the ultimate entrance by abseiling from the outside of a ten-storey building, surprising all the children being treated there. True heroes.

YOU WILL NEVER REGRET BEING KIND

HUMAN KINDNESS
HAS NEVER
WEAKENED THE
STAMINA OR
SOFTENED THE FIBRE
OF A FREE PEOPLE.
A NATION DOES NOT
HAVE TO BE CRUEL
TO BE TOUGH.

FRANKLIN D. ROOSEVELT

Ways to be kind

Volunteer to help out with an event or offer your skills to a local company whose work you admire. Perhaps you could help them set up or improve their social media accounts, or you could flyer an upcoming event for them. Or, go the traditional route and volunteer to take on a regular shift at a charity shop for a cause you support.

*Your acts of kindness
are iridescent wings of
divine love, which linger
and continue to uplift others
long after your sharing.*

RUMI

When Madalyn Parker sent an email around to her co-workers to let them know she was taking time off for her mental health, some were taken aback by her honesty. However, the CEO of her company commended her for setting such a positive example to the rest of the business, and thanked her for breaking through the stigma around mental illness. What a great reminder to be kinder to ourselves, as well as to others.

ONE KIND ACT
CAN CHANGE
SOMEONE'S DAY

WHEN YOU ARE
KIND TO SOMEONE IN
TROUBLE, YOU HOPE
THEY'LL REMEMBER AND
BE KIND TO SOMEONE ELSE.
AND IT'LL BECOME
LIKE A WILDFIRE.

WHOOPI GOLDBERG

Ways to be kind

Say hi to someone who's alone at a work event or a social function. They may be a lone wolf, but most people will appreciate some company if they're otherwise going to be alone.

Love one another and you will be happy. It's as simple and as difficult as that.

In 2013, Dan Black was raising money to fund a stem cell operation that would help him walk again, after a cycling incident left him badly injured. While he was fundraising, he heard about a five-year-old boy called Brecon Vaughan, whose cerebral palsy meant that he had only ever walked with the aid of a frame. Dan decided to give the entire £22,000 he had raised to Brecon, which helped pay for the life-changing operation to help him walk unassisted – an incredible and selfless decision.

ASK YOURSELF
THREE
QUESTIONS
BEFORE
YOU SPEAK:
IS IT TRUE?
IS IT
NECESSARY?
IS IT KIND?

I've been searching for ways to heal myself, and I've found that kindness is the best way.

LADY GAGA

Ways to be kind

If you spot something that makes you think of someone you love, send them a photo of it to let them know you're thinking of them. Or, better yet, send it to them in the post (if it's small enough, of course!). This works equally well if you spot an inspirational article you think they'd love, or have come across a comedian who's had you in stitches – share the links, and spread the joy.

CARE ABOUT
THE BEINGS YOU
CARE ABOUT IN
GORGEOUS AND
SURPRISING WAYS.

ÄNNE HERBERT

When a Brazilian transgender student, Maria Muniz, was fined for wearing a skirt to school, a group of classmates made a stand by wearing skirts themselves. Both male and female students at the school supported Maria's decision to wear what felt comfortable, and as a result of the protest the school agreed to reassess their uniform policy. Maria was touched by the support of her peers, and hoped that it set an example to students around the world.

Kindness is always possible

ALWAYS
BE A LITTLE
KINDER THAN
NECESSARY.

J. M. BARRIE

Ways to be kind

If, like lots of us, you have a problem with portion sizes and often end up cooking way too much food, why not share it with a neighbour who lives alone, or who you know isn't much of a cook? An unexpected delivery of a Tupperware full of stew or curry — or even some leftover cake if you can bear to part with it — will be the loveliest surprise.

*Seek to do good
and you will find
that happiness will
run after you.*

JAMES FREEMAN CLARKE

When two-year-old Brody Allen was diagnosed with brain cancer, his family was told he only had weeks left to live. His parents were devastated that their son wouldn't make it to Christmas – his favourite holiday – so decided to give Brody one last festive season. Once the rest of the community heard about Brody's final Christmas, they all decided to get involved, decorating the whole neighbourhood so that he could enjoy the most wonderful time of the year (just a little ahead of schedule).

START MIXING WITH YOUR OWN *KIND-A* PEOPLE

KIND HEARTS ARE
THE GARDENS. KIND
THOUGHTS ARE THE ROOTS.
KIND WORDS ARE THE
BLOSSOMS. KIND DEEDS
ARE THE FRUITS.

HENRY WADSWORTH LONGFELLOW

Ways to be kind

Leave positivity notes for strangers to find. A scribbled "Have a nice day!" or a beautifully calligraphic "You look great today" left pinned to a signpost or tucked in the pages of a library book is sure to make the person who discovers it smile.

There are
always flowers
for those who want
to see them.

HENRI MATISSE

It was in the qualifying heat of the 2016 Rio Olympics 5,000 m race when two runners made the headlines, but not for their sporting achievements. New Zealand's Nikki Hamblin and America's Abbey D'Agostino had a collision over halfway round the track, causing D'Agostino to trip up and sustain a foot injury. Instead of Hamblin returning to the race to compete for a spot in the next round, she turned back and helped her competitor all the way to the finish line. Now that is sportsmanship at its finest.

THE FIRST
RULE FOR
FEELING GOOD:
MAKE OTHERS
FEEL GOOD

How far that little candle throws his beams! So shines a good deed in a naughty world.

WILLIAM SHAKESPEARE

Ways to be kind

Pay it forward! Imagine how amazing you'd feel if you went to buy your regular coffee or to pay the bill in a restaurant, and found out someone in front of you had paid for your order. Why not give that gift to someone else today? If you're in no position to go buying people dinner, you could slip a few spare coins into a vending machine or arcade game to surprise the next person who comes along.

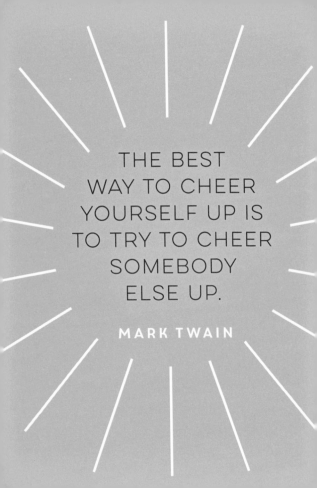

THE BEST
WAY TO CHEER
YOURSELF UP IS
TO TRY TO CHEER
SOMEBODY
ELSE UP.

MARK TWAIN

In 2020, while wildfires ravaged most of southern Australia, a team of Muslims from the Australian Islamic Centre decided to provide freshly cooked meals for the firefighters tackling the blaze. What's more, the group also distributed several batches of emergency supplies and resources across the affected region. Another group in the same area, from Sikh Volunteers Australia, set up a mobile kitchen to feed both firefighters and bush fire evacuees, providing invaluable support and comfort to those affected.

A BIG
HEART
=
A GOOD
LIFE

LET US BE
GRATEFUL TO
THE PEOPLE
WHO MAKE US
HAPPY; THEY ARE
THE CHARMING
GARDENERS WHO
MAKE OUR SOULS
BLOSSOM.

MARCEL PROUST

Ways to be kind

Offer to mentor someone, whether it's professionally or in sharing a skill you have. Time is our most valuable commodity, after all, so showing someone that you're prepared to spend time on a regular basis to help them achieve their goals is one of the most effective ways to make a positive impact on someone's life. Everyone has something they can offer to others, whether it's expertise in something technical in your job or passing on your DIY skills to the next generation.

Great opportunities
to help others seldom
come, but small ones
surround us every day.

SALLY KOCH

Donut City – a doughnut shop in California – has been run by John and Stella Chhan for over thirty years. When customers noticed that Stella hadn't been working in the shop for a while, John let them know that his wife was recovering from an aneurysm. Patrons of the store, deciding that John should be able to spend more time with his wife, started a campaign on social media to sell out the store as fast as possible every day – and it worked, with the store selling out sometimes as early as 7 a.m. Stella is now happily back behind the counter.

See the
good in
everyone

COMPASSION IS THE GREATEST FORM OF LOVE HUMANS HAVE TO OFFER.

RACHEL JOY SCOTT

Ways to be kind

We're quite often in a position to help someone, but miss those opportunities because we're not actively looking for them. Maybe you're at the beach and overhear the person next to you saying they've run out of sunscreen — you could offer to share yours. Let someone stand under your umbrella while you wait for the bus. Or offer that person who's just spilled tea down themselves a tissue. There are opportunities to spread kindness all around us.

**Do your little bit
of good where
you are; it's those
little bits of good
put together that
overwhelm the world.**

DESMOND TUTU

In 2018, online comedian Carlos Davis and his brother spotted a woman paying for her fuel in small change. Thinking that she may want help, the brothers approached and offered to pay the cost for her. Immediately, the woman burst into tears. It transpired that her husband had died the week before, so the act of kindness meant more to her than ever. When asked why he helped, Carlos said, "It's only right, we've got to stick together."

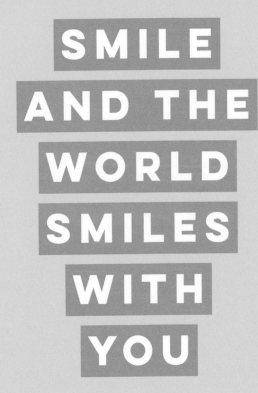

That best portion
of a good man's life;
his little, nameless,
unremembered
acts of kindness
and of love.

WILLIAM WORDSWORTH

Ways to be kind

Next time you're invited to a friend's house for dinner or to a party, offer to help tidy up at the end. The fact you haven't just rushed off as soon as the fun's over will mean a lot to the host.

GOODNESS
IS THE ONLY
INVESTMENT
THAT NEVER
FAILS.

HENRY DAVID
THOREAU

In Perth, Australia, in 2014, a man tripped as he was about to board a train and got his leg trapped in the gap between the platform and the carriage. Despite his efforts, he wasn't able to dislodge it. But help came from hordes of fellow commuters who all teamed up to push the train away from the platform and help free his leg. The moment was caught on CCTV and is a recorded tribute to the kindness of strangers.

KINDNESS IS
WORTH MUCH
MORE THAN GOLD

JOY COMES
NOT THROUGH
POSSESSION
OR OWNERSHIP,
BUT THROUGH
A WISE AND
LOVING HEART.

BUDDHIST PROVERB

Ways to be kind

Let someone go in front of you in the queue — just because. Take the extra time that you spend waiting to meditate or to practise mindfulness, or to bask in the pleasure of having made someone else happy.

Feeling gratitude and not expressing it is like wrapping a present and not giving it.

WILLIAM ARTHUR WARD

When Cameron Lyle was 19 years old, he signed up to be a bone marrow donor. He thought nothing more of it until, when he was 21, he received a message saying that he was a 100 per cent match for a 28-year-old man with leukaemia. At the time, Cameron was a college athlete and at the top of his game. However, in a selfless act of sacrifice, he chose to cut his sporting career short in order to donate his bone marrow and save the life of a stranger.

BEING KIND IS THE SIMPLEST WAY TO MAKE THE WORLD A BETTER PLACE

**TREAT OTHERS
AS YOU WOULD
LIKE OTHERS
TO TREAT YOU.**

THE GOLDEN RULE

Ways to be kind

Forgive. Being kind isn't always about doing something active to help others — sometimes it's allowing ourselves to think more kindly about them and appreciate their side of things. Give the person who wronged you the benefit of the doubt, and try to think up charitable explanations for why they might have acted in a way that upset you. If you can think on them with kindness and assume the best, rather than the worst, you'll benefit from the peace of mind it brings, and it'll allow you to treat them with more kindness in the future. A win-win!

The meaning of life is to find your gift. The purpose of life is to give it away.

ANONYMOUS

Bookcrossing.com is a website that encourages readers to "release their books into the wild" for a stranger to find. The principle is simple: once you've finished with a book, you leave it in a public place for someone else to find and enjoy. You can do this anywhere, of course, but the website means you can track where your book ends up and watch your book travel the world – spreading kindness from person to person, one book at a time.

Kindness nourishes the mind, body and soul

We can't help
everyone, but
everyone can
help someone.

RONALD REAGAN

Ways to be kind

Support other people's endeavours. If someone you know is trying something new — maybe they're venturing into the world of amateur dramatics, they've set up a social club, or they've just joined a band — turn up to support their efforts and make sure you clap along!

HOW
WONDERFUL IT
IS THAT NOBODY
NEED WAIT A
SINGLE MOMENT
BEFORE STARTING
TO IMPROVE
THE WORLD.

ANNE FRANK

Seven-year-old Jase Hyndman sent a birthday card to his late father. It was addressed: "Mr. Postman, can you take this to Heaven for my Dad's birthday?" To his family's surprise, a few weeks later they received a response from Sean Milligan, the post service's Delivery Office Manager. Sean assured Jase that the letter had been safely delivered, and that "it was a difficult challenge avoiding stars and other galactic objects en route to Heaven". Jase's family say that the act of kindness has restored their faith in humanity.

#BEKIND

CONCLUSION

Hopefully reading the incredible stories collected here will have reminded you of all the goodness in the world, and perhaps even inspired you to plan some random acts of kindness of your own. Each one of the people in this book carried out a selfless deed that will, in turn, have generated countless others. Imagine the immense power we have to transform our world for the better, simply by looking for opportunities to spread goodwill and help others as often as we can. All it takes is a little kindness.

If you're interested in finding out
more about our books, find us on
Facebook at Summersdale Publishers and
follow us on Twitter at @Summersdale.

www.summersdale.com

IMAGE CREDITS

pp.6, 21, 36, 51, 66, 81, 96, 114, 126, 141, 156
© StockVectorIllustrations/Shutterstock.com

pp.10, 15, 20, 25, 30, 35, 40, 45, 50, 55, 60,
65, 70, 75, 80, 85, 90, 95, 100, 105, 110,
115, 120, 125, 130, 135, 140, 145, 150, 155
© Rebellion Works/Shutterstock.com

pp.16, 31, 46, 61, 76, 91, 106, 121, 136,
151 © Supza/Shutterstock.com